"Love God
with your
whole heart,"

says the Lord

....

received

The Blessed Eucharist

for the first time

Church ....

on the ....

CHILD OF GOD

PRAYER BOOK

FOR

BOYS & GIRLS

Revised and expanded
by

Dr. Kelly Bowring, S.T.D.

With original text by
Fr. Daniel A. Lord, S.J.

Published by:
Willam J. Hirten Company
Cumberland R.I.
New York

ACKNOWLEDGEMENTS

Original Imprimatur:
Francis J. Spellman, D.D.
Archbishop of New York
1942

Nihil Obstat:
Reverend John Cush, S.T.L.
Diocesan Censor

Imprimatur for Revised Book:
Most Reverend Nicholas DiMarzio, Ph.D., D.D.
Bishop of Brooklyn

Brooklyn, New York
April 28, 2006

DEDICATION

*This revised book is dedicated
to the memory of...*

Fr. Daniel A. Lord, S.J.

He was a true...

Companion of Jesus
&
Defender of Youth

TABLE OF CONTENTS

WHEN I GO TO MASS

Every Sunday I go to Holy Mass.
Often during the week I go to Mass, too.
Mass is a wonderful thing.
Jesus is present in Mass.
He prays for me.
He asks His Father in Heaven to take
  care of me.
He asks me to help Him give gifts to
  God.
You see God gave us everything.
But I am so small, I do not have much
  to give Him.
But at Mass I have wonderful things to
  give to Him.
I give Him my heart by listening to
  His Word.
I help the priest give Him bread and
  wine with thanks and praise.
Bread and wine are what people use to
  stay alive.
So we give them to God.

That means I would like to give Him
my life.
Jesus will change the bread and wine
into His Body and Blood.
The priest says, "This is My Body."
And the bread becomes the Body of
Jesus.
The priest says, "This is My Blood."
And the wine becomes the Blood of
Jesus.
The priest does this because Jesus told
him to.
Then I will offer to God, with everyone
else, His dear Son Jesus Christ.
We say to God in Heaven,
"Please accept the Body and Blood of
Your dear Son."
God is glad to receive that Gift.
Then I join everyone in giving myself
to God.
We say, "When You take Your dear
Son, please take us, too.

God does and is happy.
He then gives us His Son in the
  Eucharist.
This is the greatest miracle!
This is what we do together at Mass.

I COME TO CHURCH

The church is a wonderful place.
Jesus Christ lives there.
His home is the little house on the altar.
We call that the Tabernacle.
I see a red light burning.
That means Jesus is in His little house.
I see the altar.
That is a very important table.
On it, the priest lays gifts for God.
From it, He brings Holy Communion to
  the people.
There are candles burning.
They mean: "Be so good that people
  will see you. You will be like a
  shining light."

They mean: "God's truth is like a bright
   light."

BEFORE MASS BEGINS

I arrive early for Mass to prepare for
   this special time with Jesus.
I get ready for the greatest of Miracles!
The priest is dressing for Mass.
The clothes he puts on we call vestments.
They are beautiful.
They make us think of Jesus Christ.

I TALK TO GOD

I say: "Dear Father, I offer You this Mass.
Please accept it. I will give You bread and
wine. That means I would like to give You
my life. I will give You Your dear Son, Jesus
Christ. I will give You myself."

Then I ask God for things. I say, "Please be good
to the entire world. Forgive sinners for
their sins. Teach everyone Your truth."

Then I pray for myself. "Please make me very good. Take care of me all my life."

Then I ask for something special. It may be anything that is good. I say, "And please give me this gift I want for myself, if it is good for me."

I remember this:

The first Mass was said by Our Lord
   Jesus Himself.
He said it at the Last Supper.
He did what the priest will do at Mass.
He offered His Father bread and wine.
He changed them into His Body and
   Blood.
He gave the Apostles Holy Communion.
He told the Apostles,
   "Do this in memory of Me."
So they said Mass, too, from then on.

14

THE PRIEST BEGINS MASS

I may begin Mass praying quietly:

*I will go to the altar of God with the
  priest in my heart.*
*For God makes me happy when I am
  praying.*
God, please take away my sins.
*I want to be good. Then, I can give
  You, dear God, gifts You will like.*

Then we say the Penitential Rite out loud:

**I confess to Almighty God,
and to you, my brothers and sisters,
that I have sinned through my own
  fault,
in my thoughts and in my words,
in what I have done,
and in what I have failed to do;
and I ask blessed Mary, ever virgin,
all the angels and saints,
and you my brothers and sisters,
to pray for me to the Lord, our God.**

Lord, have mercy.
Christ, have mercy.
Lord, have mercy.
Amen.

THE PRIEST GOES UP TO THE ALTAR

I may pray quietly to the Saints to help me:

Dear God, I am going to pray with my
    heart.
I am going to help the priest say Mass.
Dear Saints, you are in Heaven
    but a little piece of your relic is in
    the altar.
Please pray for me to God.
I want to love Him and serve Him as
    you did.

THE "GLORIA"

This is a beautiful prayer of joy. It was first sung by the Angels on Christmas night. We sing it, too. For Christ will soon come again in Mass. I glorify and bless the Holy Trinity with all my love.

We pray joyfully:

**Glory to God in the Highest,
And peace to His people on earth...**

**Lord Jesus Christ, only Son of the
   Father...**

**You alone are the Lord...
   in the glory of God the Father. Amen**

THE PRIEST READS THE PRAYER
   OF THE DAY

I quietly offer the Mass to God with him.

*Dear God, I give You this Mass.
Please give us the grace we need.
Please bring us safely to Heaven.
Amen.*

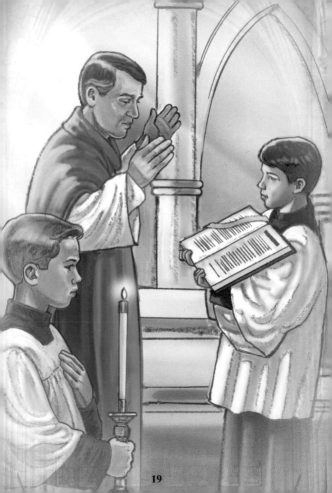

LITURGY OF THE WORD

THE READINGS AND
RESPONSORIAL PSALM

I must pay attention to the holy readings. The procla-mation of God's Word is always centered on Christ. Old Testament writings prepare for Him; New Testament books speak of Him directly.

The second reading is usually part of a letter. One of the 'Great Apostles of Jesus' wrote these long ago. They knew Our Dear Lord very well. So they wrote to their friends about Him. They told their friends all about Jesus.

So I may say quietly:

Dear Apostles, Peter, Paul, John...
Teach me about Jesus Christ.
You knew Him so well.
You loved Him so much.
Tell us about Him.
I want to know Him, too.
And love Him as you did.

THE PRIEST READS THE GOSPEL

Gospel is a word that means "Good News."
The Good News is the story of Our Dear Lord. So the Gospels tell about Jesus. They tell how He was a little baby in Bethlehem. They tell what He said. They tell the wonderful things He did. They tell how kind He was and sweet to everyone. They tell how He died for me. They tell how He rose from the grave, and lives forever.

I will tell the Lord that I am here to listen, and that I want Him to speak to my heart today:

Dear God, I want to know all about
   Jesus.
He was the greatest Man that ever lived.
He is Your Son.
He is God, the Second Person of the
   blessed Trinity.
I shall listen to His teachings.
Then I may become like Him.
That will make me kind and good.
That will make me holy.

After the Gospel, the priest gives a homily. He tells
me about the readings from the Bible and how to
understand them. I must pay attention to the entire
homily, and remember it for the rest of the day. The
Word of God will transform me into a Saint.

On Sundays and Holy Days, we pray the Creed. This
is a great Act of Faith. It was written a long time ago.
It shows that we know the truth. It says that we have
listened to Jesus Christ. It means that we believe in His
Church.

We believe in one God,
  the Father, the Almighty, ...
We believe in one Lord, Jesus Christ,
  the only Son of God, ...
Through him all things were made. ...
  He came down from heaven: ...
by the power of the Holy Spirit ...
  born of the Virgin Mary ...
  crucified under Pontius Pilate; ...
  died and was buried.
  On the third day He rose again ...
  he ascended into heaven
  and is scated at the right hand
  of the Father.

He will come again in glory to judge
   the living and the dead, ...
We believe in the Holy Spirit ...
   who proceeds from the Father ...
   He is worshiped and glorified.
He has spoken through the Prophets.
We believe in one holy catholic
   and apostolic Church
We acknowledge one baptism
   for the forgiveness of sins.
We look for the resurrection
   of the dead, and the life
   of the world to come. Amen.

*Then, we unite to pray for today's needs of the Church
and the world. We pray the Prayers of the Faithful.*

I join in, saying:

Lord, hear our prayers.
Amen.

LITURGY OF THE EUCHARIST

PREPARATION OF THE ALTAR
AND THE GIFTS

We have been fed by God's Word. Now we will enter into the Eucharistic Sacrifice itself. We celebrate the memorial the Lord instituted at the Last Supper. Now the priest uncovers the chalice. He offers to God the bread which we call the Host. He pours wine and water into the Chalice. He offers this to God.

Then I may pray quietly:

Please take, O dear God, these gifts.
We offer you bread and wine.
We could not live without bread.
So bread is important for life.
Please take this bread and wine.
But really, we want to give You our lives.
We want to live for You.
We want to work for You.
When we die, we want to go to You in
*   Heaven.*
Lord, I offer You all that I am and all
*   that I have.*

I put everything into Your Hands.
By the merits of Your Son, transform
    me, God Almighty.

AT THE WASHING OF THE HANDS

The priest washes his hands. He wants to show us we must wash our soul of all evil and sin.

So I may pray quietly:

I will wash my soul, too.
Please wash away from my soul
    any bad or evil things I've done.
I won't do them again.

The priest turns to us. He asks us to help him say the prayers. I do help Him.
I may pray quietly.

Please accept this Mass, dear Father.
The Angels sing to You.
I know they are here carrying my
    offerings and prayers before Your
    Altar.
The Saints pray to You.

29

May they pray for me.
I offer You this Mass.
I will join them.
I want to be like the Angels and the
  Saints.
I offer You my sorrows, my hopes, my
  joys, my prayers.
I know the Mass has infinite value.
I ask for the conversion of sinners, for
  peace in the world, for my family,
  for my neighbors, for all who need
  prayer.

The priest leads the Sanctus prayer. In this prayer, he
does this: he asks all to think of what takes place. He asks
us to join the Angels and Saints in calling to God and prais-
ing Him.

Holy, holy, holy Lord...

I may also say this prayer quietly:

I am Your child, dear God.
So I should love You.
And I should tell You that I love You.

That is what the Angels do when they
   sing.
That is what the Saints do when they
   praise You.
So I ask the Angels and Saints to help
   me.
I know Mary is kneeling behind the
   priest, ready to worship her Son.
I know the blessed souls of Purgatory
   are here awaiting my prayers for them,
   so they can go to Heaven sooner.
And to You, dear God, I say:
You are good.
You are holy.
I kneel before You to worship You.
I want You to come to me soon.
Please come very soon.

THE CONSECRATION

*The priest now begins the most holy part of the Mass.
During this, we pray for everyone. The priest asks me to
pray for everyone too.*

As I pay attention to the prayers of the priest, I may also pray quietly:

Dear God, please be good to us all.
Lots of people don't know about Your
    Son, Jesus.
Please let me know.
Lots of people do wicked things.
Please don't let them.
Bless everyone.
Make good people better.
Make strong people stronger.
Help our Holy Father, the Pope.
Help our Bishop and our priests.
I know You are here in the priest.
My parents have been good to me.
Will You please be good to them?
Help and bless my teachers.
And give gifts to everyone I love:
    my brothers and sisters, my
    relatives, my playmates and friends.

The Altar Server may ring the bell. This is to tell us that Jesus is coming. Soon He will be on the altar.

The bread will be turned into His Body. The wine will be turned into His Blood. Jesus will want me to be glad He has come.

So I may pray quietly:

Dear Jesus, soon You are coming.
You said, "This is my Body."
You said, "This is my Blood."
You would not tell me a lie.
I believe what You said.
And I am so glad You are coming.

*The priest bends over the altar. First, he takes the bread. He does what Our Lord told him to do: He says, **"This is My Body"** Then he lifts our dear Lord's Body high above his head.*

I may look up and say quietly:

My Lord and my God.
Jesus, I am so glad You have come to me.
I love You. I look upon You with love.
I see Jesus Crucified in the Eucharist.
I am at the foot of Calvary with Mary.

*The priest takes the chalice of wine. He does what Our Lord told him to do: He says, "**This is My Blood**" Then he lifts the chalice of Our Lord's Blood high above his head.*

I may look up and say quietly:

My Jesus, thank You very much for
   being with me.
You are my God and my All.
Your will be done.

The priest now continues the Eucharistic Prayer. He is talking to God in Heaven. He is talking to our Lord on the Altar. But he wants us to talk to God, too.

The priest prays for the dead. Many people die every day. Sometimes our relatives and friends die. Some go right to Heaven, but some do not. They have small sins on their souls. They go to Purgatory to be cleansed of their sins. They need our prayers. They want to go to Heaven soon. They can go sooner if I pray for them.

So now I may pray quietly:

Please do not leave my friends in
   Purgatory.

Take all in Purgatory soon to Heaven.
They want to be happy.
They will be happy when they come to
* Heaven.*
Please, Jesus, take them there very
* soon.*

The priest prays:

Through him,
with him,
in him,
in the unity of the Holy Spirit,
all glory and honor is yours,
almighty Father,
for ever and ever.

Amen.

*After the Great '**Amen**', the priest leads us in the 'Our Father'. This is the perfect prayer. Jesus taught it to us:*

Our Father who art in Heaven,
hallowed be thy name;
Thy kingdom come;
Thy will be done on earth
as it is in heaven.
Give us this day our daily bread;
and forgive us our trespasses
as we forgive those who trespass
against us;
and lead us not into temptation,
but deliver us from evil.

Then I may also pray:

I forgive all who have hurt me.
Give them my peace God.
Please don't let any harm happen to me.
Keep me from sin.
Keep evil far away from me.
I want to stay with You, dear Jesus.
When I am with You, I am safe.

To welcome the Lord, we pray for forgiveness and exchange a sign of peace. Before receiving Jesus, we must be united with Him and with the Saints in Heaven, the souls in Purgatory, and everyone in the world.

The priest bends over the Body and Blood of Jesus. We pray the "Agnus Dei" prayer. Agnus Dei means Lamb of God. It is the name St. John the Baptist used for Jesus. Lambs were gifts given to God. They were killed for the sins of the people. Jesus is our Gift given to God. He was killed on Calvary. Jesus cannot die again. But we can give Him to God. So the Mass is Calvary represented. The Crucified Jesus is made present on the Altar.

Lamb of God, You take away the sins of the world,
have mercy on us.
Lamb of God, You take away the sins of the world,
have mercy on us.
Lamb of God, You take away the sins of the world,
grant us peace.

I may also pray quietly:

Dear little Lamb of God,
Jesus Christ,
Who died on Calvary,
  save me from sin.
Please don't let me sin.
Please keep me white and pure like You.
Bless this priest, make him holy and
  pure. Love all the priests, Lord.

Now we get ready for Holy Communion. When we love anyone, we want to be near them. Jesus loved us very much. He wanted to be near us. He said, "What comes closest to people? Their food!" He said, "I will come as close to them as their food."

So He took bread, which is food. He said, "This is My Body." The bread became His Body, but it still looked like bread, so we could take it into ourselves. Thus, Jesus comes very close to us. We call this Holy Communion. I must get ready to receive Jesus.

So I may pray quietly:

Dear Jesus, You want us to be happy.
You don't want anything to hurt us.
You want us to be at peace.
If You are with us, we are safe.
Please come to me in Holy Communion.
I am weak. You are strong.
I do evil things.
You never did anything bad.
But You want to be with me.
You want to help me.
Please come into my heart.

I join everyone in praying to be worthy to receive Jesus:

Lord, I am not worthy to receive you,
  but only say the Word and I shall be
  healed.

48

HOLY COMMUNION

The priest receives Holy Communion. First, he takes the dear Body of Our Lord. He bows and receives the Eucharist. Then, he takes the cup of Our Lord's Blood. He bows and drinks. Jesus is with him.

Perhaps I have made my First Communion. If so, I can receive Holy Communion too. I know that Jesus wants to come to me. Very soon He will come. So I ask Him to come. I go up to receive Jesus in the Eucharist.

I may pray quietly:

I know that This is Your Body and
  Your Blood, Your Soul and Divinity.
I know this because You said it was so.
I love You very much.
You have made Yourself a Prisoner of
  Love in my heart.
Please come and be with me.
I need You very much.
I am so weak. You are so strong.
You are always good.
You await my love, and for love You
  remain with me.
I love You, Jesus.
Thank You for giving Yourself to me.

I quietly take Him into my heart. After, I go back to my pew, I talk to Him quietly with love.

Perhaps I have not received my First Communion. If not, I can receive my Spiritual Communion. I can tell Jesus I wish He would come. And though nobody can see it happen, He will come to my soul.

If I have not received First Holy Communion yet, I can pray:

Dear Jesus, I am not old enough yet.
I have not received my First
    Communion.
But I do want You to come to me, please.
I believe This is Your Body and Blood.
I love You very much.
Please come and stay with me?

After Holy Communion, I may pray quietly:

Thank You very much for coming to
    me, Jesus.
Now I have another gift to give Your
    Father and mine.
I want to give myself.

I am just a child.
But fathers love children.
So I give my Father myself.
I shall be good.
I shall be obedient to my parents.
I shall work hard at school.
I shall be kind to my playmates.
You want these gifts from me.
I give them all to You.
I am now Your image and likeness.

In the Concluding Rite, the priest blesses and dismisses the people.

As I listen to him, I may also pray quietly:

May the blessing of Almighty God,
Father, Son, and Holy Spirit,
*   rest in my body and soul forever.*
May I receive this blessing from the
*   priest as if it is the last I will receive.*
I receive this blessing in the Name of
*   the Holy Trinity.*
I make the Sign of the Cross as if it
*   was the last one of my life.*

The priest leaves the Altar. I should try not to leave my pew until he has gone. It is impolite to rush out of Church. I should also stay a minute after Mass to thank God.

I ask Him to stay with me all day:

Jesus, make this whole day holy.
You are a member of my family.
You are my closest Friend.
Let me experience the sweetness of
   Your Presence all day.

After Mass, I stay a few minutes to cherish Jesus, saying:

O Sacrament most holy,
O Sacrament divine,
All praise and all thanksgiving,
Be every moment Yours. (say 3 times)

I adore You eternally in the most
   Blessed Sacrament of the Altar

AFTER I LEAVE THE CHURCH

Jesus wants to stay with me always.
He will stay with me unless I don't
    want Him to.
He will only leave me if I am very bad.
I will never be very bad.
So when I go out of Church,
    Jesus goes with me.
He will stay with me all day.
I can turn to Him and ask for help.
His Spirit helps me.
His strength is mine.

I WILL BE VERY GOOD

All day I will be very good.
I will say, "Jesus came to me this
    morning."
He is still with me.
I will ask Him to keep me good.
I will ask Him to help me.
I will try to be like Him.

WHY DAILY PRAYER IS IMPORTANT

Before you begin to pray, always
   remember:
You are God's little child.
He is very close to you.
He sees you and hears all that you say.
He loves you very much.
He will give you what you ask for,
   if it is good for you.
When you pray, you are simply
   talking to God with devotion.
God is three divine Persons in One Being.
   He is your Father God.
   He is Jesus, God's Son, your
      dearest Brother.
   And He is God the Holy Spirit,
      Who shows you God's love.
So prayer is easy. You pray everyday.
Fathers love to speak with their children.
Children love to talk to their fathers.
God is waiting to listen to your prayer.

OUR FATHER
WHO ART IN HEAVEN

THE LORD'S PRAYER:
THE OUR FATHER

This prayer is the most important prayer Jesus gave us. This is the most perfect prayer. It is the summary of the whole Gospel. Jesus says to me, "Ask and you will receive." I pray this prayer with my heart many times a day.

OUR FATHER WHO ART IN HEAVEN

God is my Father. He is everyone's
Father.
He says to call Him *Abba*, Daddy!
He made my body and my soul.
He gave me everything good.
He made me to know Him, to love
Him, and to obey Him.
He wants me to come to Him some
day in Heaven.
There I shall be very happy with Him
and the Saints forever.

HALLOWED BE THY NAME

This means I hope everyone will love
my Father in Heaven.
I want them all to say kind things
about Him and to praise
His holy Name.
I hope everyone will know Him.
I hope they will all love Him as I do.

THY KINGDOM COME

I am a little Catholic. I love Jesus.
I belong to God's Kingdom. Besides
being patriotic, I am also a Christian.
I wish everyone was Catholic too.
They would get so many gifts from God.
They would know so many things to
make them happy.
They would know that God loves them, too.

THY WILL BE DONE ON EARTH

My Father wishes everyone to be happy.
He wishes them to be good.
He wishes them all to come to Heaven.
I hope this happens.
I hope that His will be done.

AS IT IS IN HEAVEN

In Heaven everyone does God's will.
That is why everyone is happy there.
There are Angels and Saints in Heaven with God.
On earth, lots of people are unhappy.
They do not do what God wants.
They commit sin.
I wish people on earth were like the
happy Saints in Heaven.

GIVE US THIS DAY OUR DAILY BREAD

My Father in Heaven gives me everything I need.
He gives me my food. He gives me my clothes.
He gives me the Sacraments of grace.
So I ask Him to keep on giving me all I need.
I know He will, if I trust in Him.

AND FORGIVE US OUR TRESPASSES

Trespasses are naughty bad things.
Trespasses are my sins. Sometimes I am naughty.
Sometimes I do evil things. These are sins.
I ask God to forgive my sins, please.
He promises He will, if I am sorry.

AS WE FORGIVE THOSE
WHO TRESPASS AGAINST US

Sometimes people are not nice to me.
They hurt my feelings.
They do unkind things to me.
But I will not be angry. I forgive them.
Then God will forgive me when I do
unkind things to Him.

AND LEAD US NOT INTO TEMPTATION

The world is full of dangers.
Sometimes bad people try to harm us.
They try to make us sin.
The evil spirits hate us too.
We ask our Father to take care of us.
We say, "Please don't let us fall into sin.
Please don't let us run into danger."

BUT DELIVER US FROM EVIL

The world is full of sad things, too.
The devil tries to trick us to do evil.
But, we do not want to sin and be sad.
We want to be happy.
So we ask God to take care of us.
Little children can be hurt easily.
But we pray to our Father.
He won't let anything hurt us.

AMEN

This is a word that ends all our prayers.
It means: "Please do this, my Father.
I hope what I ask will take place."
Then I say the "Hail Mary."

HAIL MARY!
FULL OF GRACE

THE HAIL MARY

Mary is my Mother in Heaven. I pray with and to Mary. She is the model of prayer. I always welcome Mary into my heart. She always leads me to Jesus and teaches me to obey Him. Jesus is pleased when I pray to Mary with love.

HAIL MARY!
This is what the Angel Gabriel said
when he visited Mary: "Rejoice!".
She was invited to be the Mother of God.
Mary was filled with joy.
She was to be the Mother of Jesus.
She is my loving Mother, too.

FULL OF GRACE
Mary was very beautiful.
She was very good.
God loved her a great deal.
She was conceived without original sin
and never committed any sin.
She always loved God completely.
He filled her soul with beautiful gifts,
with His grace; this is God's life in her soul.

THE LORD IS WITH THEE

God the Father loved Mary. She was
His daughter.
God the Holy Spirit loved her like His Bride.
God the Son loved her too.
He was sent to dwell in her in a special way, to
become her Son.
She became the Mother of Jesus.
She gave Him to the world:

BLESSED ART THOU AMONG WOMEN

This is what Saint Elizabeth, Mary's
cousin, said to her.
There have been many beautiful
women who lived.
There have been many holy people
and good people.
But Mary was the greatest of them all.
She believed fully in God's Word.

AND BLESSED IS THE FRUIT
OF THY WOMB

The fruit of her womb is her Baby. His Name is Jesus.
He is the Son of God. She is His Mother. This makes
Mary and her Baby very blessed.

JESUS

This is the Holy Name of God's Son. Jesus is divine; He
is God's Son. He also became man, when He became
Mary's Baby. She loved Him very much, and so do I.
The holy names of Jesus and Mary are at the heart of
prayer. These two names are the most powerful and
simple prayer I can pray.

HOLY MARY, MOTHER OF GOD

Mary was very good and holy.
But what made her great was this:
She became God's Mother.
For Jesus is God.
And she is the Mother of Jesus.
So she became the Mother of God.

PRAY FOR US SINNERS

When I do naughty bad things,
I become a sinner.
Mary is my Mother. She loves me
even when I am bad. So she prays for me.
She says, "Please, Jesus, my Son,
forgive my child."
And He does forgive me.
She teaches me to trust in Jesus.

NOW AND AT THE HOUR OF OUR DEATH AMEN

I need Mary's prayers now.
She is my Mother of Mercy.
These prayers keep me from being hurt.
I shall also need them when I die.
Her prayers for me will take me safely
to Heaven forever.

THE HOLY TRINITY

THE GLORY BE

Another important prayer is this prayer of praise to God. God is One divine Being in Three Persons, and He has existed forever. I should speak to Each Person of God as my Friend. In this prayer, I praise and thank the Trinity for making the world. I also look forward to being with God forever in Heaven, where I will go someday if I love Him.

Glory be to the Father,
and to the Son,
and to the Holy Spirit.
As it was in the beginning,
is now,
and ever shall be,
world without end. Amen.

WHEN I RISE FROM BED

As the day begins, my Mom and Dad call me to get up. I love my parents, so I do what they ask. Then I talk to God, my Father in Heaven, and to Mary, my heavenly Mother. I also begin my day by kneeling before the Crucifix, saying "Good Morning" to Jesus my Lord. I always begin prayer by blessing myself, making the Sign of the Cross, saying:

"In the Name of the Father, and of the Son, and of the Holy Spirit. Amen."

PRAYERS FOR RECONCILIATION

Why Do I Go to Confession?

God wants me to be good.
If I obey Him, I will be happy.
But the devil wants me to be bad.
Wicked people sometimes want me to
   be bad too.
Silly, stupid people sometimes try to
   make me do wrong things.
But, these wrong things are sins.
When I hurt my parents, I am sorry.
And I tell them I am sorry.
I say, "Please forgive me."
Then I try to do something to please
   them.
When I sin, I hurt God the Father in
   Heaven.
I hurt my heavenly Mother , Mary, too.
So I must say, "I am sorry.
   Please forgive me."
And then I try to do something to
   please them.

I say special prayers. I am very kind to
  everyone for them.
I go to confession to be forgiven of my
  sins.

**Our Dear Lord, Jesus, Started
  Confession**

Jesus knows I am weak.
Often I do things that are bad.
He wants me to get rid of these bad
  things.
He wants me to be good once more.
So He gave His Apostles wonderful
  powers.
He told them they could forgive sins.
He said to them: "Whose sins you shall
forgive, they are forgiven."
So they forgave others' sins.
And they gave that same power to
  all the bishops and priests.

THE SACRAMENT OF RECONCILIATION

Now I am ready to go to Confession. Many people may be going to Confession. If so, I stand and wait my turn. I am quiet and thoughtful. I pray to make a good Confession. When I enter the Confessional, I see if the priest is ready. I can go to him face to face or behind a screen.

When the Priest Is Ready, I Say:

Bless me, Father, for I have sinned. It has been _____ (how long) since my last Confession.
Then I tell him my sins since my last Confession.

I say what I have done that is wrong. I tell him how many times I did it.

I Say:

I was unkind to my little brother three times.
I did not say my morning prayers twice.
(Or whatever your sins were.)

ACT OF CONTRITION

**I am sorry for these and all the sins
of my whole life…
especially …** *(And I may tell a sin
of my whole life.)*

The priest then talks to me. He says:
Jesus is speaking to me through the priest. He then asks
me to make the Act of Contrition to show God I am sorry.
I pray this prayer:

**My God,
I am sorry for my sins with all my
heart.
In choosing to do wrong
and failing to do good,
I have sinned against You,
Whom I should love above all things.
I firmly intend, with Your help,
to do penance,
to sin no more,
and to avoid whatever leads me to sin.
Our Savior Jesus Christ
suffered and died for us.
In His Name, my God, have mercy.**

I Listen

The priest then pronounces that Jesus forgives my sins. God has the power to forgive my sins. He gave that power to His priests. The priest says the beautiful words of absolution and he blesses me. When he is finished, my sins are forgiven. The priest tells me I can go in peace. I thank the priest.

Then I Do Something Nice for God

God has forgiven me my sins. I want to show Him I am thankful. I do this by doing my penance. These are the prayers or good deeds the priest told me to say. This is called Penance. Really, they are a gift I give to God, to show Him I am thankful.

After I Say These Prayers
To Thank God

God, thank You for forgiving me.

I am happy again.

I will try to be good.

I will stay away from people who are
bad or mean.

I will try to do what my parents want.

God, You will help me.

You love me and want me to be good.

Thank You God. I love You.

THE MOST HOLY ROSARY

The Most Holy Rosary of the Blessed Virgin Mary is one of the most important prayers of the Church. It is a meditation on the lives of Jesus and Mary. It is a prayer that is a summary of the whole Gospel. With the Rosary, I go to the school of Mary to contemplate the Face of Christ. I will ask my parents to help me to pray the Rosary often, even daily. I should use my Rosary beads.

To pray the Rosary:
I begin by praying the 'Apostles' Creed',
  3 'Hail Marys', and a 'Glory Be.'
Then I pray an 'Our Father', 10 'Hail
  Marys', a 'Glory Be', and an 'O My
  Jesus' for each of the five mysteries.

O MY JESUS PRAYER

O my Jesus, forgive us our sins.
Save us from the fires of hell.
Lead all souls to Heaven,
Especially those in most need of Your
  mercy.

JOYFUL MYSTERIES

Pray on Mondays & Saturdays

1. The Annunciation
Luke 1:26-38

St. Gabriel appears to
Mary. He says, "Hail, full
of grace." She is invited
to be the Mother of Jesus.

2. The Visitation
Luke 1:39-56

Mary visits her cousin,
Saint Elizabeth. Elizabeth
says to her, "Blessed are
you among women."

3. The Nativity
Luke 2:1-14

Jesus is born in Bethlehem. Shepherds adore Him.

4. The Presentation
Luke 2:29-32

Mary and St. Joseph bring Jesus to the Temple. Mary was told she would suffer with her Son.

5. The Finding of the Child Jesus in the Temple
Luke 2:48-52

When Jesus was twelve, His parents lost Him at the Passover feast. He was in the Temple for 3 days.

MYSTERIES OF LIGHT

Pray on Thursdays

1. The Baptism of Jesus
Matthew 3:13

St. John the Baptist baptizes Jesus when He was about 30 years old. The Holy Trinity was revealed.

2. The Miracle at Cana
John 2:1-12

At this wedding, Mary says about Jesus: "Do whatever He tells you." Jesus turns water into wine.

3. The Kingdom of God
Mark 1:14-2:17

Jesus preaches the Gospel.
He calls all to repent and
convert. He came to heal
& save repentant sinners.

4. The Transfiguration
Luke 9:28-36

Jesus goes to a mountain
to pray with His Apostles.
Moses and Elijah appear.
Jesus is filled with light.

5. The Last Supper
Matthew 26:17-35

Jesus institutes the
Holy Eucharist and
the priesthood the
night before He died.
He tells His Apostles
to love one another.

SORROWFUL MYSTERIES

Pray on Tuesdays & Fridays

1. The Agony in the Garden
Matthew 26:38

After the Last Supper,
Jesus went to the garden to
pray. He prayed to His
Father: "Your will be
done."

2. The Scourging at the Pillar
John 19:1

Pontius Pilate had Jesus
beaten with whips. Jesus
will soon die. He said:
"No greater love is there
than to lay down one's life
for another."

3. The Crowning with Thorns   Mark 15:16

The cruel soldiers mocked Jesus. They dressed Him in purple, crowned His Head with thorns, and put a reed in His Hand. They spit on Jesus.

4. The Carrying of the Cross   John 19:17

Jesus had to carry His Cross to Calvary. St. Simon helped Him carry it. and St. Veronica wiped His Holy Face with love.

5. The Crucifixion
Mark 16:6-8

Jesus is nailed to the Cross. He forgave His killers. He told St. John to take care of His Mother. He died.

GLORIOUS MYSTERIES

Pray on Wednesdays & Sundays

1. The Resurrection
Mark 16:6-8

On the third day, Jesus
rose again from the dead.
He appeared to His disci-
ples. Alleluia!

2. The Ascension
Acts 1:10-11

Forty days after His resurrection, Jesus ascended
into Heaven. He will
come again to judge us.

3. The Pentecost
Acts 2: 1-4

After Jesus' Ascension,
Mary and the Apostles
waited for the Holy Spirit.
He came on Pentecost.

4. The Assumption
Song of Songs 2:3-6

At the end of her earthly
life, Mary was taken by
God, full body and soul
into Heaven. She is there
with Jesus.

5. The Coronation
Revelation 12:1-2

Jesus is the King of kings.
Mary is crowned the
Queen of Heaven and
earth, of all Saints and
Angels.

OUR LADY
OF THE ROSARY

HAIL, HOLY QUEEN

Hail, Holy Queen, Mother of mercy, our
  life, our sweetness, and our
  hope!
To you do we cry, poor banished children
  of Eve; to you do we send up our sighs,
  mourning and weeping in this valley of
  tears.
Turn then, most gracious advocate, your
  eyes of mercy toward us; and after this
  our exile, show unto us the blessed fruit
  of your womb, Jesus.
O clement, O loving, O sweet Virgin
  Mary!

Pray for us, O Holy Mother of God.
That we may be made worthy of the
  promises of Christ.

THE ST. MICHAEL PRAYER

St. Michael, the Archangel,
   defend us in battle;
   be our protection against the
   wickedness and snares of the devil.
May God rebuke him,
   we humbly pray;
   and do you, O Prince of the
   Heavenly Host,
   by the power of God,
   cast into hell,
   Satan and all the other evil spirits,
   who prowl about the world,
   seeking the ruin of souls. Amen.

I want to receive the special graces of
   the Church for praying the Rosary. These are
called indulgences.
So I finish my Rosary by praying for
   the Pope and his intentions.
I pray one 'Our Father', one 'Hail Mary',
   and one 'Glory Be' for the
   Pope's intentions.

THE WAY OF THE CROSS

Our dear Lord, Jesus Christ, died for all
of us.
He died because we were sinners.
As sinners, God would have to punish us.
I would never get to go to Heaven.
Because I have done evil things.
Instead, Jesus said, "Father, please punish
me instead of them.
Please let me take the place of my
sinful little brothers and sisters."
So God the Father agreed.
Jesus was hung upon a cross and died for
me.
I was the sinner, but He suffered in my
place.
I was the one who did wicked things; He
died for me.
He died on Calvary.
The evil people nailed Him to the Cross.
That was on Good Friday.

But before that, He carried His Cross a long way.

This is called the Way of the Cross.

He did this in a city called Jerusalem, a long way from here.

People go to that city to remember what Jesus did for them.

They are called Pilgrims.

They pray along the Way of the Cross.

They remember how our dear Lord had made that same journey.

They are sorry for their sins.

Now, in all our churches we can make the Way of the Cross.

Or I can do it at home, too.

I can remember how Jesus suffered for me.

I can tell Him I am sorry.

I can help Him to carry His Cross.

I can thank Him for dying for me.

PRAYER BEFORE A CRUCIFIX

Look down upon me,
  good and gentle Jesus.
Before Your Face I humbly kneel,
  and with burning soul,
  I pray and beg You to fix deep in
  my heart the lively grace of faith, hope
  and charity.
Give me true contrition for my sins
  and a firm purpose of amendment.
I contemplate with great love and
  tender pity Your five wounds,
  while I call to mind the words which
  David Your prophet said of You, my
  Jesus:

**"They have pierced my hands and
feet – I can count all my bones"** (Psalm
22:16-17).

FIRST STATION
JESUS IS TOLD BY PILATE
THAT HE WILL DIE

Before each station, we pray:

V. We adore You, O Christ, and
   we bless You.

**R. Because by Your holy Cross,
   You have redeemed the world.**

Quietly I think:

That Jesus was not a sinner.
He did nothing but good.
Yet Pilate said, "Take Him away and
   nail Him to a cross."
Jesus said nothing. He knew if He didn't
   die, I would have to go to Hell.
So He said, "Let Me die for their sake."

Quietly I pray:

Thank you very much, dear Jesus.
Because of sin, I should suffer.
Instead, You suffered for me.
I am sorry for the sins that made
   You die.
I promise You I will not sin again.

*After each station, we pray the Our Father,
the Hail Mary, the Glory Be and:*
   "May the souls of the faithful departed
through the mercy of God rest in peace."

SECOND STATION
THE SOLDIERS PLACE A HEAVY CROSS ON JESUS' SHOULDER

We pray:

V. We adore You, O Christ, and
   we bless You.

**R. Because by Your holy Cross,
   You have redeemed the world.**

Quietly I think:

That Cross is very heavy indeed.
It is made of strong, heavy wood.
But it is heavier because it is really
   made of my sins.
And they are heavy and hurt Our Lord.
But He takes the Cross gladly.
He wants to die for love of me.

Quietly I pray:

Dear Lord, make me hate sin very
   much.
I hate it because it hurt You so deeply.
I hate it because it hurts me.
I don't want to lay my sins on your
   shoulders.
I won't sin again.

*We pray the Our Father, the Hail Mary, the
Glory Be and this:*
   "May the souls of the faithful departed
through the mercy of God rest in peace."

THIRD STATION
JESUS FALLS FOR THE FIRST TIME UNDER HIS CROSS

We pray:

V. We adore You, O Christ, and
   we bless You.

**R. Because by Your holy Cross,
   You have redeemed the world.**

Quietly I think:

The Cross is very heavy.
Jesus is sick and weary.
For before this, the soldiers whipped
  Him.
And put a crown of thorns on His Head.
So now He falls under the Cross.
How heavy my sins must be!
They then knocked Jesus to the ground.

Quietly I pray:

I am so sorry, dear Jesus that You suffer.
Let me help You to rise again.
Don't ever let me fall into sin again.
You are weak because my sins hurt you
  so.
Because men were so cruel to You.
Please let me to be strong.
Please let me love You a lot.

*We pray the Our Father, the Hail Mary, the
Glory Be and this:*

   "May the souls of the faithful departed
through the mercy of God rest in peace."

FOURTH STATION

JESUS MEETS HIS DEAR MOTHER

We pray:

V. We adore You, O Christ, and
we bless You.

**R. Because by Your holy Cross,
You have redeemed the world.**

Quietly I think:

Mary loved her Son very much.
She did not want Him to suffer.
On the way to His death she meets Him.
She sees the soldiers, the Cross, His pain.
She knows He is doing this because He
     loves sinners.
She suffers with Him.
She is willing to let Him die for me.

Quietly I pray:

Dear Mother, I am sorry that I made
     you suffer too.
You hurt when you saw your Son.
You wished you could help Him.
But the soldiers would not let you.
Your Son is dying for love of me.
Please help me to love Him and to
     love you too, my Mother.

*We pray the Our Father, the Hail Mary, the
Glory Be and this:*

     "May the souls of the faithful departed
through the mercy of God rest in peace."

FIFTH STATION
SIMON HELPS OUR LORD
TO CARRY HIS CROSS

We pray:

V. We adore You, O Christ, and
we bless You.

**R. Because by Your holy Cross,
You have redeemed the world.**

Quietly I think:

The soldiers were afraid Jesus would
   die before He got to Calvary.
So they stopped a traveler they did not
   know.
His name was Simon.
At first, he did not want to help Jesus.
The soldiers made him do it.
But then he was glad he helped Jesus.
Simon became a saint.

Quietly I pray:

Dear Jesus, may I help You carry Your
   Cross?
I do this when I am kind to others.
When I am obedient to my Mother and
   Father.
When I resist sin and am very good.
I would like to be a little saint too.

*We pray the Our Father, the Hail Mary, the
Glory Be and this:*

   "May the souls of the faithful departed
through the mercy of God rest in peace."

SIXTH STATION
VERONICA WIPES THE FACE
OF JESUS WITH HER VEIL

We pray:

V. We adore You, O Christ, and
we bless You.

**R. Because by Your holy Cross,
You have redeemed the world.**

Quietly I think:

There was a holy woman in the crowd
  named St. Veronica.
The rest of the crowd hated Jesus.
But she wanted to help Him.
She took her veil from her head and
  wiped His face.
On the veil, Jesus left a beautiful
  picture of Himself.

Quietly I pray:

Dear Lord, I wish I could help You too.
And I can, even now. So, I will!
If other people hate You, I will
  love You more.
If they don't believe in You, I will
  believe in You.
I offer You my heart.
Please put Your image on it forever.

*We pray the Our Father, the Hail Mary, the
Glory Be and this:*

  "May the souls of the faithful departed
through the mercy of God rest in peace."

SEVENTH STATION
JESUS FALLS A SECOND TIME
UNDER HIS CROSS

We pray:

V. We adore You, O Christ, and
we bless You.

**R. Because by Your holy Cross,
You have redeemed the world.**

Quietly I think:

Jesus is very weak.

The Cross gets heavier and heavier.

Jesus falls again.

The soldiers hit Him and make Him
get up.

This fall hurts Him very much.

Quietly I pray:

Dear Jesus, I'm so sorry for this fall.

I know why it happened.

That is because people fall into sin so
often.

They promise to be good and then sin
again.

They go to Confession and then go
right back to sin.

Don't let me fall into sin.

Let me stand up strong and pure.

*We pray the Our Father, the Hail Mary, the
Glory Be and this:*

"May the souls of the faithful departed
through the mercy of God rest in peace."

EIGHTH STATION
JESUS SPEAKS TO THE WOMEN
WHO WEEP FOR HIM

We pray:

V. We adore You, O Christ, and
   we bless You.

**R. Because by Your holy Cross,
   You have redeemed the world.**

Quietly I think:

Some holy women were in the crowd.
Jesus blessed their babies for them.
He had been good to them.
Now they see Him suffering so much.
They are sorry that their Friend is
   suffering.
Jesus answers them: "Don't cry over Me.
   Cry over yourselves and your little
   children."

Quietly I pray:

Dear Jesus, I should be crying because
   You are in such pain.
And because You are dying for my sins
   and for me.
So I say, "Forgive me for my sins that
   hurt You so. Please don't ever let me
   sin again."

*We pray the Our Father, the Hail Mary, the
Glory Be and this:*
   "May the souls of the faithful departed
through the mercy of God rest in peace."

NINTH STATION
JESUS FALLS FOR THE THIRD TIME UNDER HIS CROSS

We pray:

V. We adore You, O Christ, and
   we bless You.

**R. Because by Your holy Cross,
   You have redeemed the world.**

Quietly I think:

How heavy the Cross is!
But Jesus falls still again.
The soldiers kick Him and beat Him
   and force Him to rise.
He heard the crowd laughing at Him
   and calling Him names.
These are the people He loves and who
   He helped all He could.

Quietly I pray:

Dear Jesus, don't ever let me cause
   You pain.
I will always say, "I believe in Jesus
   Christ, my Lord".
I will always tell people that I am Your
   little child.
I will always do what I am supposed to.
Thus, I'll help You carry Your Cross.

We pray the Our Father, the Hail Mary, the Glory Be and this:

   "May the souls of the faithful departed
through the mercy of God rest in peace."

TENTH STATION
THE SOLDIERS TAKE AWAY JESUS' CLOTHES

We pray:

V. We adore You, O Christ, and
   we bless You.

**R. Because by Your holy Cross,
   You have redeemed the world.**

Quietly I think:

They all reach the top of the hill.
The soldiers throw the Cross on the
  ground.
Then they tear away Jesus' clothes.
The crowd looks at Him in that cruel way.
They take away from Him everything,
  even His cloak His Mother made Him.

Quietly I pray:

Jesus, so many people are immodest
  and impure.
You are suffering for them.
So many people are greedy; they want
  everything.
You are suffering for them too.
Let me always be modest and pure.
Let me always love You more than
  anyone or anything.

*We pray the Our Father, the Hail Mary, the
Glory Be and this:*

  "May the souls of the faithful departed
through the mercy of God rest in peace."

ELEVENTH STATION

JESUS IS NAILED TO THE CROSS

We pray:

V. We adore You, O Christ, and
we bless You.

**R. Because by Your holy Cross,
You have redeemed the world.**

Quietly I think:

They threw our Lord down on the Cross.
They took heavy nails and drove them
    into His hands and His feet.
They lifted Jesus on the Cross.
There He hung suffering terribly.
He said to His Father: "Father, forgive
    them; I give You My life for them."
He did, and our sins were forgiven.

Quietly I pray:

Dear Jesus, I thank You so much.
I should have suffered for my sins.
Instead, You died upon the Cross for
    me and for the whole world.
Father, I offer to You Your Son.
He hangs there in my place.
Forgive me my sins and never let me
    sin again.

*We pray the Our Father, the Hail Mary, the
Glory Be and this:*

    "May the souls of the faithful departed
through the mercy of God rest in peace."

TWELFTH STATION

JESUS DIES ON THE CROSS

We pray:

V. We adore You, O Christ, and
we bless You.

**R. Because by Your holy Cross,
You have redeemed the world.**

Quietly I think:

Jesus hung on the Cross for three hours.

He was very thirsty; but they only gave
   Him vinegar to drink.

He gave us His Mother to be our
   Mother.

He takes the Good Thief St. Dismas with
   Him to Heaven as He dies.

He has won for us the right to go to
   Heaven too.

He won the forgiveness of our sins.

Quietly I pray:

Thank you, dear Jesus, so much.

You forgave me and died for me.

You gave me Your Mother, and I love
   her.

And in Mass, I can offer You up every
   day.

*We pray the Our Father, the Hail Mary, the
Glory Be and this:*

   "May the souls of the faithful departed
through the mercy of God rest in peace."

THIRTEENTH STATION
JESUS IS TAKEN DOWN
FROM THE CROSS

We pray:

V. We adore You, O Christ, and
we bless You.

**R. Because by Your holy Cross,
You have redeemed the world.**

Quietly I think:

Jesus has died.

A soldier pushes a spear into His Sacred Heart.

The earth shakes and darkens.

Then His dead body is taken from the Cross.

His Mother takes her dead Son in her arms, and she cries.

Quietly I pray:

Dear Mary, you must have been so sad.

You remembered Jesus when He was young, and you remembered Him when He was a strong man.

Now He is dead and in your arms.

I am sorry that sin killed Him.

Please protect me from sin.

Mary, please be with me when I die.

We pray the Our Father, the Hail Mary, the Glory Be and this:

"May the souls of the faithful departed through the mercy of God rest in peace."

FOURTEENTH STATION

JESUS IS LAID IN THE TOMB

We pray:

V. We adore You, O Christ, and
we bless You.

**R. Because by Your holy Cross,
You have redeemed the world.**

Quietly I think:

Jesus was so poor that He did not own
 a grave.
So a rich man gave Him his grave.
Mary wrapped Him carefully.
The Holy Women, St. John, and the
 rich man carried Him to the grave.
But after three days He rose again!
He was strong and beautiful.
He lived again forever.
This was the first Easter.

Quietly I pray:

Dear Jesus, some day I too shall die.
I am not afraid.
When I die, I shall not stay in the
 grave; I shall follow You.
You rose from the dead; so shall I.
I shall go to Heaven with You.
Thank You very much indeed!

*We pray the Our Father, the Hail Mary, the
Glory Be and this:*

 "May the souls of the faithful departed
through the mercy of God rest in peace."

AFTER THE STATIONS

I Now Promise God to lead a Good Life:

Lord Jesus, I promise to be a good
   Catholic.
I shall never sin again.
I shall never give in to temptation.
I shall never say: "I am not a Catholic; I do
not believe in Jesus Christ."
I shall do my studies well.
I shall be obedient and sweet at home.
I shall try to help others to be better.
I shall try to make others know You,
   and love You too…
Help me! I know that You will.

*Then I say the 'Our Father', the 'Hail Mary', and
the 'Glory Be' for our Holy Father, the Pope, and
his intentions.*

PRAYER TO YOUR
GUARDIAN ANGEL

Angel of God, My guardian dear,
To whom his love Commits me here;
Ever this day (or night)
Be at my side, To light and guard,
To rule and guide. Amen.

THE TEN COMMANDMENTS OF GOD
God's Law of Love, Grace and Freedom

I. I am the Lord your God...
You shall have no other gods before me.

God made us to know, love, and serve Him and to be happy with Him forever in Heaven. Jesus, You are my one Lord and God, and I love You.

THE TEN COMMANDMENTS OF GOD
God's Law of Love, Grace and Freedom

II. You shall not take the name of the Lord your God in vain.

We must honor God's holy Name and only speak His Name with reverence and praise. Jesus, Jesus, Jesus – I honor Your Holy Name.

THE TEN COMMANDMENTS OF GOD
God's Law of Love, Grace and Freedom

III. Remember to keep holy the Sabbath day.

From the beginning, God has taught us to rest one day a week. As Catholics, Sunday is a special day of rest and prayer with our families, especially by going to Mass. Lord, help me to worship You by always going to Mass on Sunday and making it a special day of prayer and rest.

THE TEN COMMANDMENTS OF GOD
God's Law of Love, Grace and Freedom

IV. Honor your father and your mother.

We must love, respect, and obey our parents.
When we obey our parents, we obey God and
please Him. Jesus, teach me to love and obey my
parents as You were obedient to your parents, Mary and
Joseph. Help my parents to guide me in Your ways.

THE TEN COMMANDMENTS OF GOD
God's Law of Love, Grace and Freedom

V. You shall not kill.

*Our lives belong to God, and we must take care of
ourselves. We must also be a good example to others and
treat them as we want to be treated.
Thank you God for my life and help me to love
everyone as You love me.*

THE TEN COMMANDMENTS OF GOD
God's Law of Love, Grace and Freedom

VI. You shall not commit adultery.

*We will be happy if we learn the virtues
of purity and modesty.
Blessed Virgin Mary and St. Joseph, help me
to be pure in all I see, hear, say, and do.*

THE TEN COMMANDMENTS OF GOD
God's Law of Love, Grace and Freedom

VII. You shall not steal.

*We must be fair and honest, we should also
share what belongs to us with others.
Jesus, I trust in You to take care of me and
to provide for my needs.*

THE TEN COMMANDMENTS OF GOD
God's Law of Love, Grace and Freedom

VIII. You shall not bear false witness against your neighbor.

*We must never harm another by saying false or
unkind things about them.
We must always tell the truth.
Lord, help me not to judge so that I will not be
judged, help me to always tell the truth
even if I may be punished.*

IX. You shall not covet your neighbor's wife.

In this commandment, God is telling us to never willingly think or do impure things. Only when a man and a woman are married can they make a family as God intends. Lord, please help all husbands and wives to love each other and help everyone to honor the Sacrament of Matrimony. Help me to be chaste and to dress modestly.

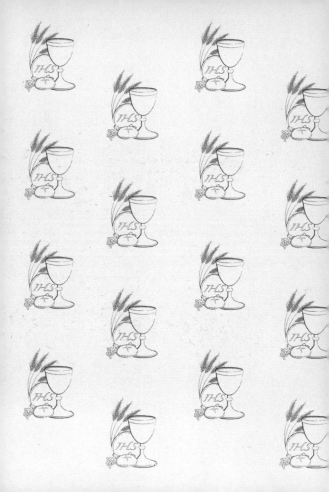